AIR MINISTRY.

Directorate of Research.

CENTRAL HOUSE,

KINGSWAY, W.C. 2.

I.C. 673.

Enemy Engine Report No. 21.

REPORT

ON THE

Transmission and Reduction Gear

OF A

Siemens Bomber.

MAY, 1919.

H. R. BROOKE-POPHAM,

Brigadier General,

Director of Research.

The Naval & Military Press Ltd

Published by

The Naval & Military Press Ltd
Unit 10 Ridgewood Industrial Park,
Uckfield, East Sussex,
TN22 5QE England

Tel: +44 (0) 1825 749494
Fax: +44 (0) 1825 765701

www.naval–military–press.com
www.military–genealogy.com

in association with

Imperial War Museums
iwm.org.uk

AIR MINISTRY.

Directorate of Research.

CENTRAL HOUSE,

KINGSWAY, W.C. 2.

I.C. 673.

Enemy Engine Report No. 21.

REPORT

ON THE

Transmission and Reduction Gear

OF A

Siemens Bomber.

MAY, 1919.

H. R. BROOKE-POPHAM,

Brigadier General,

Director of Research.

REPORT OF THE TRANSMISSION AND REDUCTION GEAR
OF A SIEMENS BOMBER.

INDEX.

LIST OF ILLUSTRATIONS.

MAIN GEAR BOX.

SECONDARY GEAR CASE.

FIG. 1.
MAIN GEAR BOX.

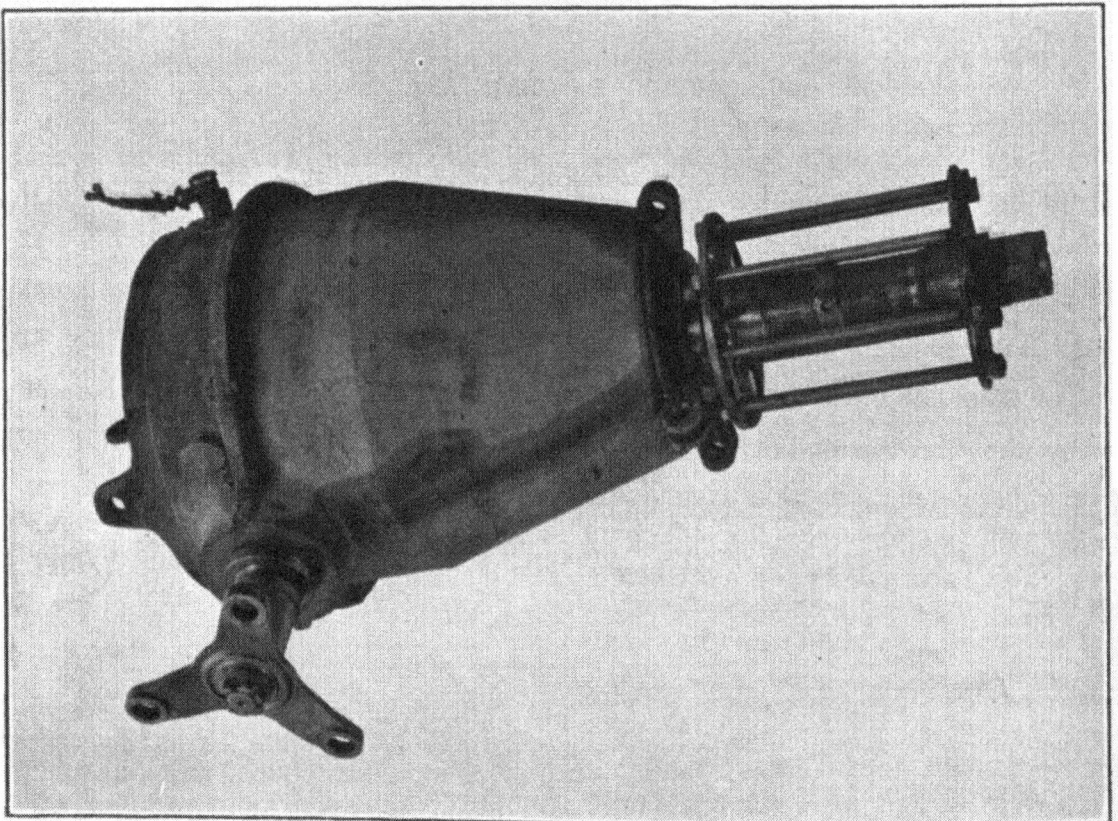

FIG. 2.
SECONDARY GEAR BOX.

Report on the Transmission and Reduction Gear of a Siemens Bomber.

INTRODUCTORY NOTE.

The following illustrated report on the design and construction of a reduction and distribution gear is based on an examination of its three units taken from an aeroplane found wrecked in an experimental aerodrome outside Cologne, in January, 1919.

The aeroplane itself was too badly damaged for reconstruction : its leading particulars are given below :—

Type	Siemens Riesenflugzeug (Giant flying machine).
Span of Top Plane	86 ft. 0 in.
Span of Bottom Plane	68 ft. 8 in.
Gap	8 ft. 6 in.
Overall Length	50 ft. 0 in.

General description.—The object of this gear is to transmit the drive from three 230 H.P. Benz engines in the fuselage to two propellers mounted between interplane struts on either side, at a speed reduction of ·638/1.

Three separate units are incorporated in the system, a main and two secondary gear boxes. The main gear box is carried in the fuselage, in which are installed three 230 H.P. Benz engines ; of these, two are located in front of and one immediately behind this gear box. The drive is through double cone clutches, the female members of which are formed in a fly-wheel mounted at the end of each crankshaft.

The secondary gear boxes are built into the interplane struts, and driven from the main gear box through lengths of shafting and flexible couplings. These gear boxes are cone shaped, and were apparently streamlined by means of aluminium cowls fitted to their rear ends.

Both the main and secondary units are of very clean design, but are on the heavy side. Bevel gear wheels are used throughout, no spur wheels being employed, and all the bearings are of the self alinging type manufactured by the Skefko Ball Bearing Company.

FIG. 3.

MAIN GEAR BOX WITH BOTTOM HALF REMOVED.

Main Gear Box.—The general lay out of the main gear box may be seen from Figs. 1, 3, 4, 16, 17, and 18. Five shafts in all are housed in this member, three driving shafts and two driven, all of which run in ball bearings housed in the casing. The latter is in two halves, the joint being along two planes inclined at 142 degrees (this being the angle subtended by the two driven shafts).

6

Both halves are aluminium castings ; the lower half, which forms the sump, is of very light design, weighing only 34·2 lbs., whilst the upper half is more substantially built. The upper halves of the various bearing housings are cast integral with this half ; studs and dowels being screwed into either

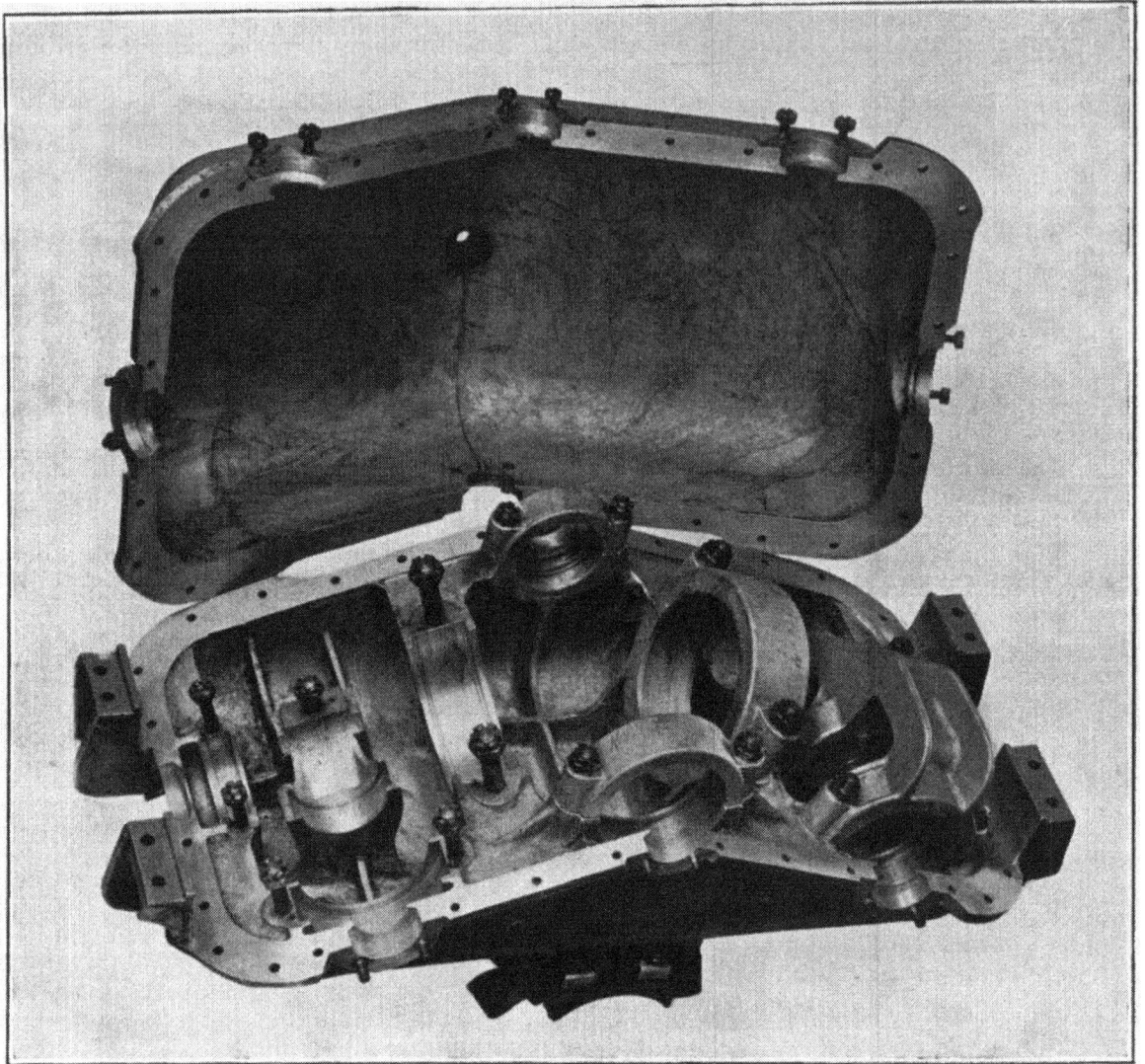

FIG. 4.

MAIN GEAR BOX WITH SHAFTS REMOVED.

side of each housing for the attachment and registration of its respective cap. The casing is well stiffened by internal webs. Two deeply webbed supporting feet, each drilled for two 13 mm. bolts, are cast at opposite sides of the case and straddle the driven shafts. A platform to which the wireless alternator (possibly) may be strapped is mounted on the forward face of the upper half, and behind this two light steel brackets, carrying pulleys, through which cable controls are reeved. The purpose of these controls as well as that of the lever mounted immediately behind then is not apparent. Two large oil filler holes are machined in the upper half, and are closed by hexagonal steel caps.

Forward Driving Shaft.—This is illustrated assembled and stripped in Fig. 5, and a cross section is given in Fig. 17. A flywheel with a hexagonal shank is machined at its forward end, whilst a 30 toothed bevel wheel, meshing with its fellow on the driven shaft, is locked by three keys to a taper machined at the rear end. This wheel is secured in position on the shaft against the inner race of its rear bearing by an annular nut screwed to the end of the shaft and locked in position by set screws. The inner race of the forward bearing is carried on the shank of the bevel wheel and retained in position against a shoulder turned thereon by an annular nut screwed to the shank, and again secured by set screws. A common cap retains the two bearings in their housings and straddles the driven shaft, being anchored to a seating immediately behind this shaft and to other seatings on either side of the forward bearing housing.

FIG. 5.

FORWARD DRIVING SHAFT [MAIN GEAR BOX].

Rear Driving Shaft.—This is illustrated assembled in Fig. 6 and in section in Fig. 16. Its design is very similar to that of the two forward shafts, the clutch end being the same in all respects. A 30-toothed bevel wheel is secured by two keys to a taper machined at its forward end, and meshes with an bevel wheel on each of the driven shafts. The inner race of the forward bearing is carried on the shank of this wheel, and both race and wheel are retained in position on the shaft by a ring nut screwed on the shaft and locked by two set screws. The end of the shaft projects through the gear box and is stepped in diameter, being machined with a key-way to form the mounting in all probability for the wireless alternator pulley.

FIG. 6.

REAR DRIVING SHAFT [MAIN GEAR BOX].

The Clutch.—This is of the double cone type in which two leather covered male cones are forced apart under the action of male and female scrolls, and are thereby engaged with their female elements which are machined in the engine fly-wheel.

The forward cone is machined from a steel pressing, and is riveted to a steel shank machined hexagonal, both internally and externally, so that when it is passed over the hexagonal part of the shaft it is virtually splined thereto.

The rear cone is of similar construction, and is mounted on the hexagonal shank of the forward cone so that both members rotate solid with the driving shaft.

The rear cone is operated by the outer member of a " muff scroll " through a ring plate bolted to the forward end of the latter. Thrust rings carried on either side of this plate transmit the axial movement of the scroll to the cone through races mounted on two sleeves screwed to its shank.

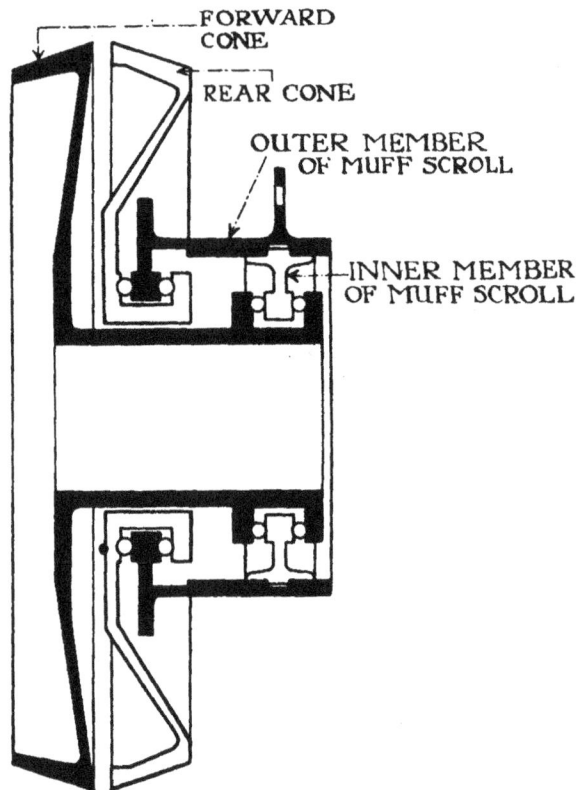

FIG. 7.

DIAGRAMATIC SECTION THROUGH CLUTCH.

The " muff scroll " is illustrated in Figs. 6 and 8 ; it will be seen that the inner member is locked against rotation, but can move axially. If, therefore, the outer member be rotated in a clockwise direction it will move backwards and the inner member will move forwards. The inner member operates the forward cone ; a thrust race mounted on either side of the diaphragm formed in its bore transmits its axial movement to the cone through two races carried on sleeves screwed to the rear end of its shank.

The fork to which the inner member of the muff scroll is anchored is bolted to the gear case, and forms the cap of the packing gland of the shaft. The flywheel machined at the forward end of the shaft has a forwardly projecting lip in which eight internal ratchet-shaped teeth are cut. The reason for these is uncertain, since the engine side of the clutch is missing ; probably some form of centrifugal dog clutch is incorporated therewith in order to prevent clutch slip at high speeds. The female member of the rear cone is bolted to the rear face of the engine flywheel, an annular ring (shown in Fig. 17) being interposed between the two members to form an anchorage for the rear cone to bear against when the clutch is being disengaged.

No external clutch springs were fitted : the clutch was operated by a hand wheel screwed to a lever pivoted to a lug projecting from the outer member of the muff scroll.

The Driven Shaft.—Fig. 9 illustrates this member stripped and assembled, a sectional view is given in Fig. 18.

The drive is transmitted to a pair of bevel wheels mounted at the inner end of the shaft, which is parallel sided. These are located radially by three keys extending the total length of the two wheels, the whole being secured by a ring nut locked by two set screws. The inner race of the main bearing of this shaft is mounted on the shanks of the two bevel wheels, being secured between collars turned on each. This race (Skefko S.K.F. 1416) is of massive design, the balls being $1\frac{1}{16}$in. diameter. The outer bearing is secured on the shaft against a shoulder turned thereon, and by a ring nut locked by means of set screws.

The outer end of the shaft passes through a packing gland, and is machined to a taper to which is keyed a three-armed spider (one element of the flexible coupling between the gear case and the shafting).

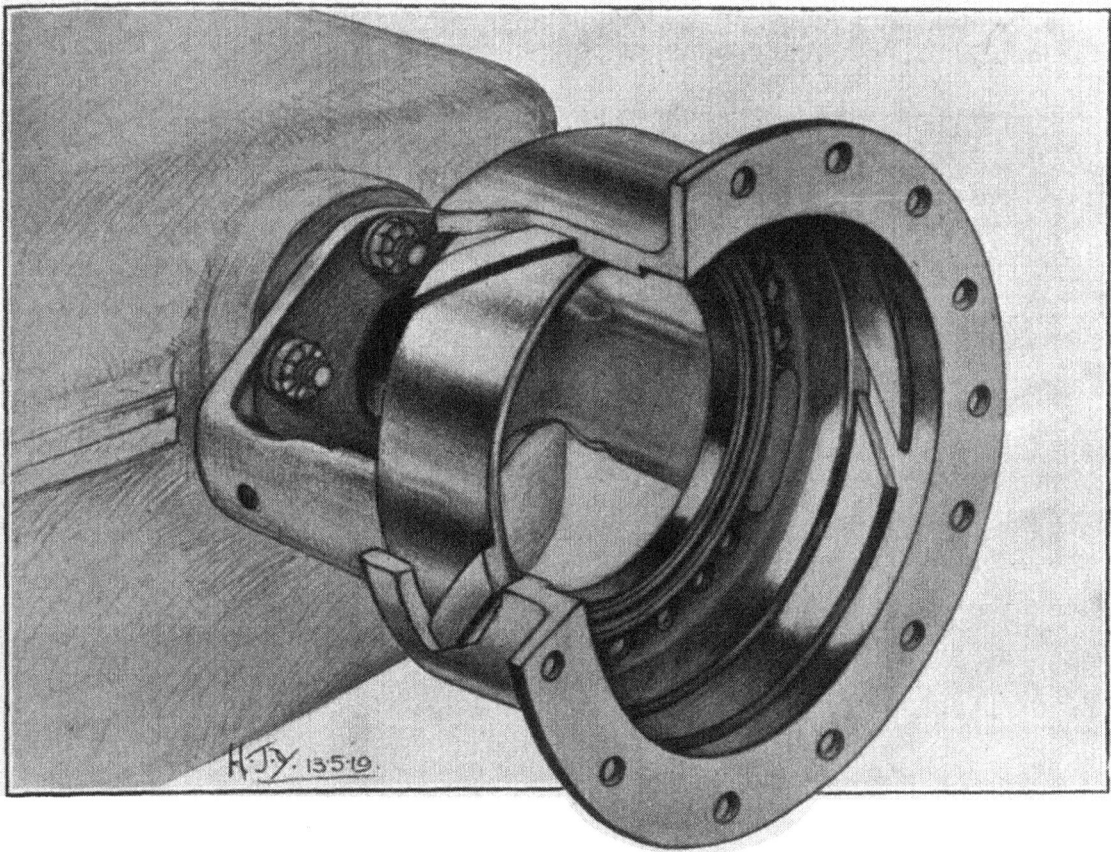

FIG. 8.
"MUFF SCROLL" OPERATING CLUTCH.

FIG. 9.
DRIVEN SHAFT [MAIN GEAR BOX].

Flexible Coupling.—This is of the disc type, two three-armed spiders being attached to the angular points of a hexagonal frame-work of laminated steel strip. Details of this coupling are given in the data at the end of the report.

FIG. 10.
SECONDARY GEAR BOX.

Secondary Gear Box.—In this unit the drive from the main casing is transferred to the propeller shaft through right angle bevel gears. Two shafts only are contained in this unit, the propeller shaft, and the driving shaft.

The gear box itself is cone shaped and is built in two parts, the rear portion being detachable and in the form of a cap ; the joint is situated across the axis of the driving shaft, and is of the usual flange type secured by bolts.

The housings for the propeller shaft bearings are both located in the forward portion of the casing, the rear bearing housing being formed in a diaphragm cast in the casing half way along its length. The forward bearing (with which is incorporated a double acting thrust race) is housed in a steel cap bolted to the forward end. The housings of the driving shaft bearings are formed between the two halves of the casing. As in the main gear case, packing glands are fitted to the ends of the propeller and driving shafts projecting from the casing ; the caps in this instance being screwed over bosses projecting from the casing and from the forward bearing housing respectively. Triangular shaped lugs which may be locked to the casing by a set screw project from these caps. The outer bearing housing of the driving shaft is closed by a screwed cap. Lugs formed on the rear portion of the casing and on a plate secured to the nose by the same bolts which attach the forward bearing housing form the means of attachment of the gear case to the interplane struts. It will be seen from the drawings that this unit may be used on either side of the machine owing to the possibility of handing the shaft.

Electrical Thermometer.—An electrical resistance thermometer consisting of a non-inductive winding of some standard high resistance wire (probably German silver), was fitted to each of the secondary units. The ends of the wire were probably connected, through a battery, to a milli-ammeter with a dial registering in degrees centigrade. The maximum temperature used would be in the neighbourhood of 16 degrees C.

If used with a standard Mark III English Lighting Accumulator giving $2\cdot2$ volts the milli-ammeter would require a range of 12 to 21 milli-amperes for a temperature range of 15 degrees to 160 degrees C. No calibration of any value can be made without knowing the voltage or the type of instrument used.

The reason for fitting this thermometer (which is illustrated in Fig. 12) is not apparent, as no provision seems to have been made for controlling the temperature of the oil.

Driving Shaft.—Fig. 11 illustrates this member both stripped and assembled. Fig. 15 gives a cross sectional view.

The drive is taken from the counter shaft through a flexible coupling similar to that used on the main gear box, a three armed spider being keyed and secured by a nut to the end of the shaft. A 35-toothed bevel wheel is keyed to the shaft which is parallel sided, immediately behind the inner race of the bearing of the driven end, and retained in position between this race and a shoulder turned on the shaft, by a nut screwed to the shaft and bearing on the race. The inner race at the further end of this shaft is secured against a shoulder turned thereon by a ring nut locked in position by two set screws.

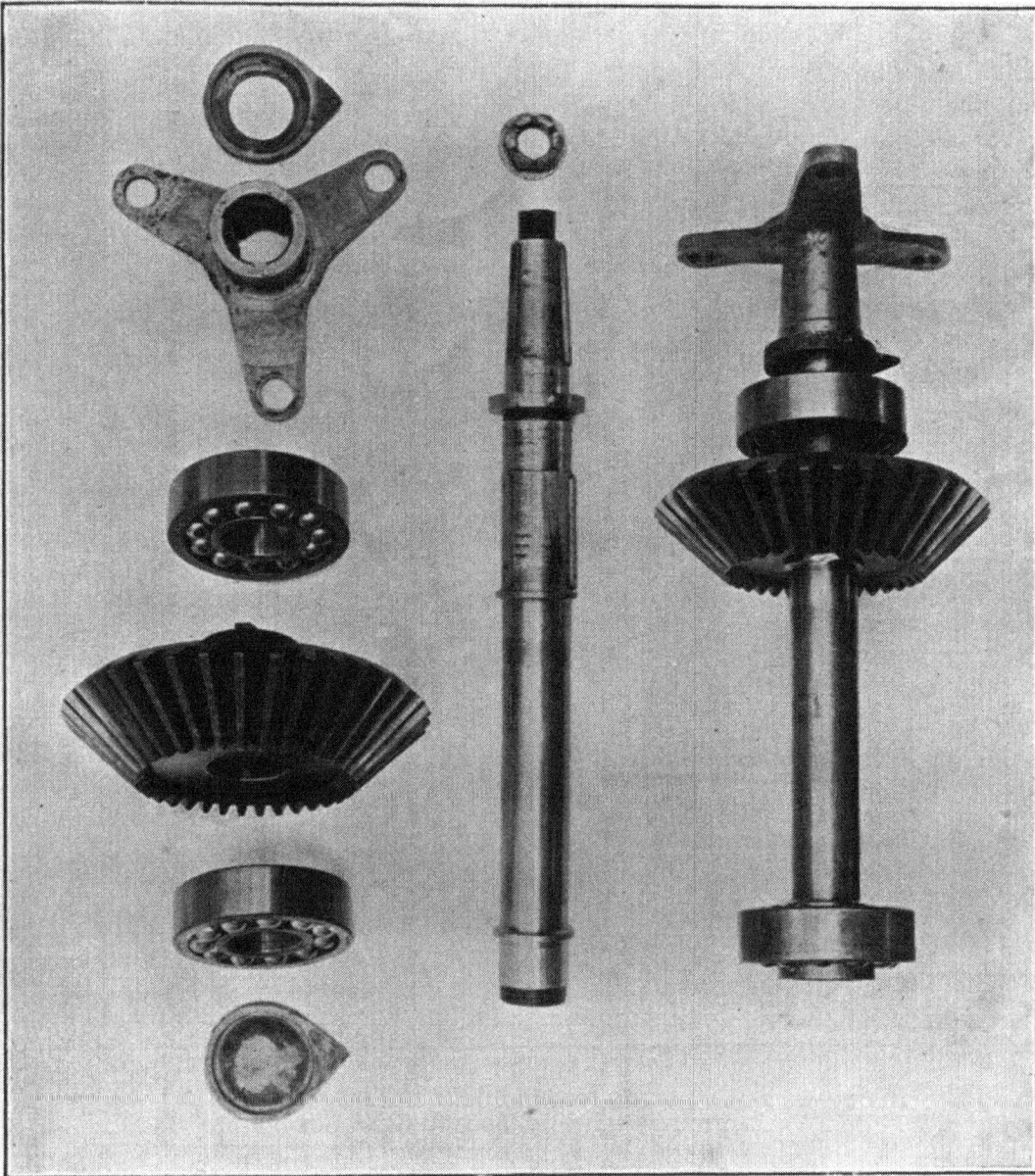

FIG. 11.
DRIVING SHAFT [SECONDARY GEAR BOX].

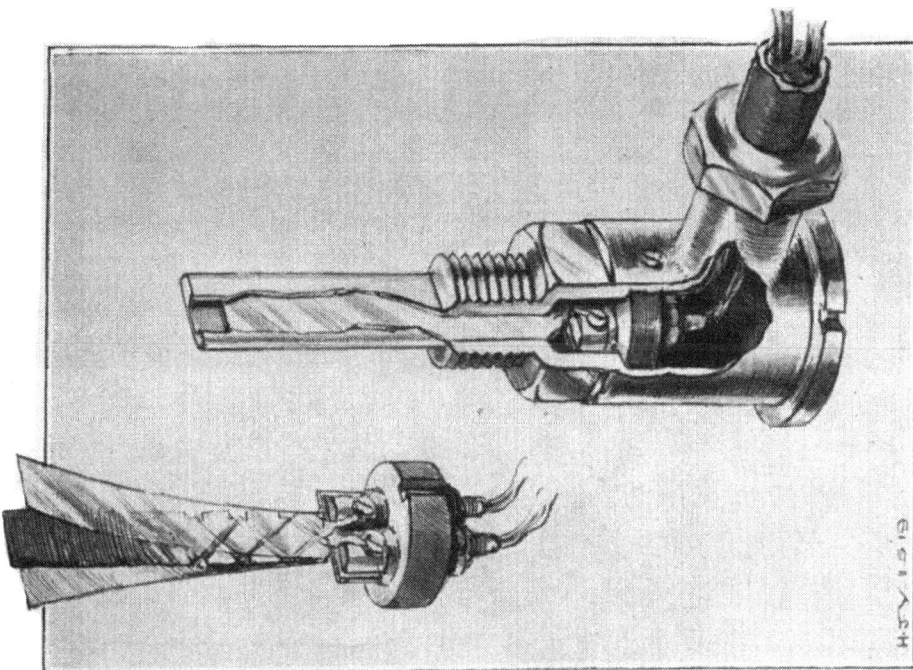

FIG. 12.
ELECTRICAL RESISTANCE THERMOMETER.

C

Fig. 13.
Propeller Shaft [Secondary Gear Box].

Fig. 14.
Thrust Race.

Propeller Shaft.—This is illustrated assembled and stripped in Fig. 13, and in section in Fig. 15. A 35-toothed bevel wheel is keyed to the rear end, which is parallel sided, and is secured against a shoulder turned thereon by a ring nut locked to the shaft by set screws. The double acting thrust race and the forward bearing are retained on the shaft between a shoulder turned on the shaft towards its forward end and two lock-nuts screwed to the shaft nearer its centre. A taper is machined on the shaft immediately in front of this shoulder to form a mounting for the propeller hub, which is secured thereto by three keys and a nut.

Thrust Race.—This is of the double-acting self-aligning type and is illustrated in Fig. 14. A common thrust ring is anchored to the shaft between two annular distance pieces. The rear distance piece is retained in position against the foremost of two lock-nuts screwed to the shaft. The second distance piece is retained against the inner race of a roller bearing which abuts against a shoulder turned on the shaft. The two outer rings are carried in a cage; the lips closing the ends of the cage are ground to form spherical seatings for the rings which are similarly ground. The two rings and sets of caged balls are assembled through two notches cut for that purpose in the rear lip of the cage. The outer race of the roller bearing and the cage of the thrust race are carried in a housing bolted to the nose piece; an annular ring screwed into the mouth of the housing and locked in position by set screws completes the assembly.

TRANSMISSION AND REDUCTION GEAR—SIEMENS BOMBER.
GENERAL DATA.

Main Gear Box.

Driving Shaft (rear) number .. .. One.

    Diameter .. .. 49 mm.

    Length .. .. 756 mm.

  Rear Bearing, type .. .. "Skefko" S.K.F. medium.

    Type number 1310

  Forward Bearing, type .. .. "Skefko" S.K.F. extra heavy.

    Type number .. .. 1412.

  Bevel Pinion, number of teeth .. .. 30.

    Module .. .. 6.

    Width of teeth .. .. 55 mm.

  Clutch, largest diameter over leather .. .. 338 mm.

    Thickness of leather .. .. 4 mm.

    Width of leather .. .. 40 mm.

    Angle of face .. .. 18 degrees.

Driving Shafts (forward) number .. .. Two.

    Diameter .. .. 50 mm.

    Length .. .. 440 mm.

    ,, of flats.. .. .. 128 mm.

    Width across flats .. .. 58 mm.

  Forward Bearing, type .. .. "Skefko" S.K.F. extra heavy.

    Type number .. .. 1412.

  Rear bearing, type .. .. "Skefko" S.K.F. extra heavy.

    Type number .. .. 1407.

  Bevel Pinion, number of teeth .. .. 30.

    Module .. .. Six

    Width of teeth .. .. 55 mm.

  Clutch, largest diameter over leather .. .. 338 mm.

    Thickness of leather .. .. 4 mm.

    Width of leather .. .. 40 mm.

    ,, across flats .. .. 72 mm.

    Length of flats .. .. 70 mm.

    Angle of face .. .. 18 degrees.

Driven Shafts, number .. .. Two.

    Included angle .. .. 142 degrees.

    Diameter .. .. 60 mm.

    Length .. .. 546 mm.

  Small Bearing, type .. .. "Skefko" S.K.F. light.

    Type number .. .. 1212.

  Large Bearing, type .. .. "Skefko" S.K.F. extra heavy.

    Type number .. .. 1416.

  Bevel wheel, number .. .. Two.

    Number of teeth .. .. 47.

    Module .. .. Six.

    Width of teeth .. .. 55 mm.

TRANSMISSION AND REDUCTION GEAR—SIEMENS BOMBER.

Flexible Coupling.

Number	4.
,, of laminations	45 mm.
Width ,, ,,	46 mm.
Thickness ,, ,,	2 mm.
Bolts, pitch circle	240 mm.
,, diameter	28 mm.
Bosses, thickness	16 mm.
Casing, thickness (average)	9 mm.
,, of flange	16 mm.
,, of cover	6 mm.
Number of bolts	30.
Diameter of bolts	10 mm.
Maximum length	416 mm.
,, width	828 mm.
,, depth	407 mm.

Secondary Gear Box.

Driving Shaft.

Length	670 mm.
Diameter (mean)	60 mm.
Bearings, number	Two.
Type	" Skefko " S.K.F. extra heavy.
Type number	1412.
Bevel wheel, number of teeth	35.
Module	Eight.
Width of teeth	80 mm.

Propeller Shaft.

Length	744.
Diameter (mean)	66.
Forward Bearing, type	" Skefko " S.K.F. light.
Type number	1215.
Rear Bearing, type	" Skefko " S.K.F. extra heavy.
Type number	1416.
Bevel Wheel, number of teeth	35.
Module	Eight.
Width of teeth	80 mm.
Propeller, Hub, diameter	80 mm.
Length between flanges (approx).	240 mm.
Flange diameter	220 mm.
,, thickness	8 mm.
,, bolts, number	8.
,, ,, diameter	14 mm.
,, ,, pitch circle diameter	190 mm.
Casing, thickness (average)	4·5 mm.
,, of cover	5 mm.
Maximum length	652 mm.
,, diameter	416 mm.
Number of bolts	12.
Diameter ,,	10 mm.

TRANSMISSION AND REDUCTION GEAR—SIEMENS BOMBER.
GENERAL ANALYSIS OF WEIGHTS.

Main Gear Box.

Casing.

	lbs.	
Upper half complete with bearing caps and auxiliary fittings	123·50	
Lower ,,	34·20	
Bolts	3·40	

Engine Shafts (3).

Short Shafts (2).

Shaft with nuts and keys	27·20	
Clutch, forward cone	12·25	
,, rear cone	11·50	
,, operating mechanism with thrust races (2)	14·55	
Anchor piece	2·10	
Bevel pinion and nut	9·40	
Large bearing	8·90	
Small ,,	3·00	
Total weight of each shaft	88·90	177·80

Long Shaft.

Shaft with nuts and keys	35·80	
Clutch, forward cone	12·25	
,, rear cone	11·50	
,, operating mechanism with thrust races (2)	14·55	
Anchor piece	2·10	
Bevel pinion and nut	9·40	
Large bearing	8·90	
Small ,,	2·75	
Total weight of shaft	97·25	97·25

Driven Shafts.

Shaft with nuts and key	17·400	
Bevel wheel	16·625	
,, ,, and bearing	36·750	
Packing gland cover	1·000	
Coupling (Spider)	7·375	
Small bearing	2·000	
Total weight of each shaft	81·150	162·30
		601·45

Secondary Gear Boxes.

Casing.

	lbs.	
Main body	63·40	
Cover	41·00	
Supporting Ring	6·25	

Driving Shaft.

Shaft with nuts and keys	17·875	
Bevel wheel	23·200	
Bearings (2 off)	17·800	
Coupling (Spider)	7·375	
Gland Nut	1·000	
		67·25

TRANSMISSION AND REDUCTION GEAR—SIEMENS BOMBER.

Propeller Shaft.

Shaft bare with nuts and keys	31·000	
Bevel wheel and nut	24·45	
Large bearing	20·00	
Small ,,	3·00	
Thrust race complete	10·38	
Distance pieces (2 off)	·80	
		89·63
Thrust housing and nuts		10·83
Propeller Hub		17·00
		295·36

Engine Fittings.

Female portion of clutch (3 off)	6·5	
		19·50
Distance rings (3 off)	1·5	
		4·50
		24·00

Accessories.

Flexible coupling plates (4 off)	7·5	
		30·00

Summary of Weights.

Main Gear Box	601·45
Secondary Gear Box	295·36
,, ,, ,,	295·36
Engine Fittings	24·
Accessories	32·
Total weight of Gear complete without shafting	1248·17

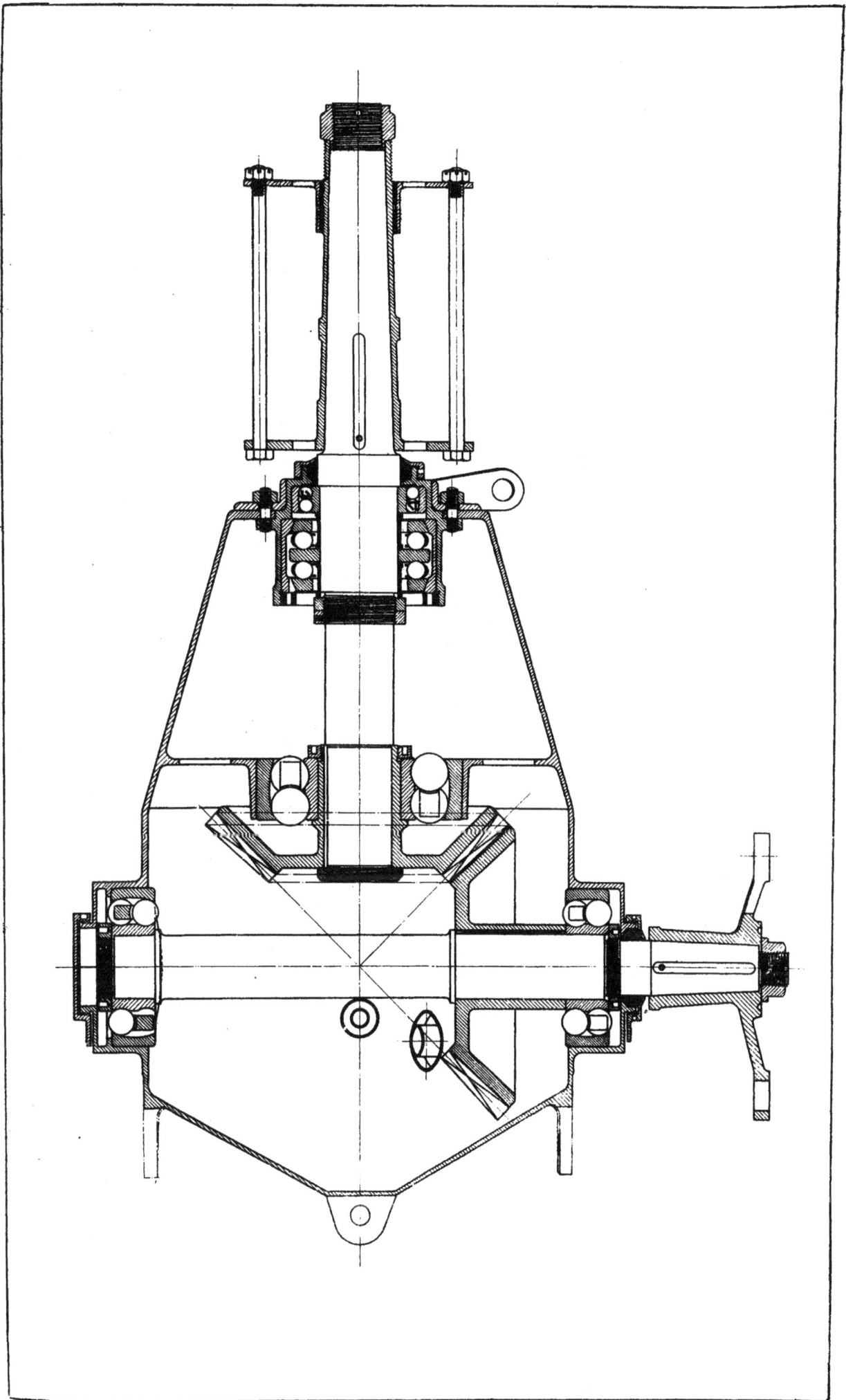

FIG. 15

<u>Longitudinal Section through Secondary Gear Box.</u>

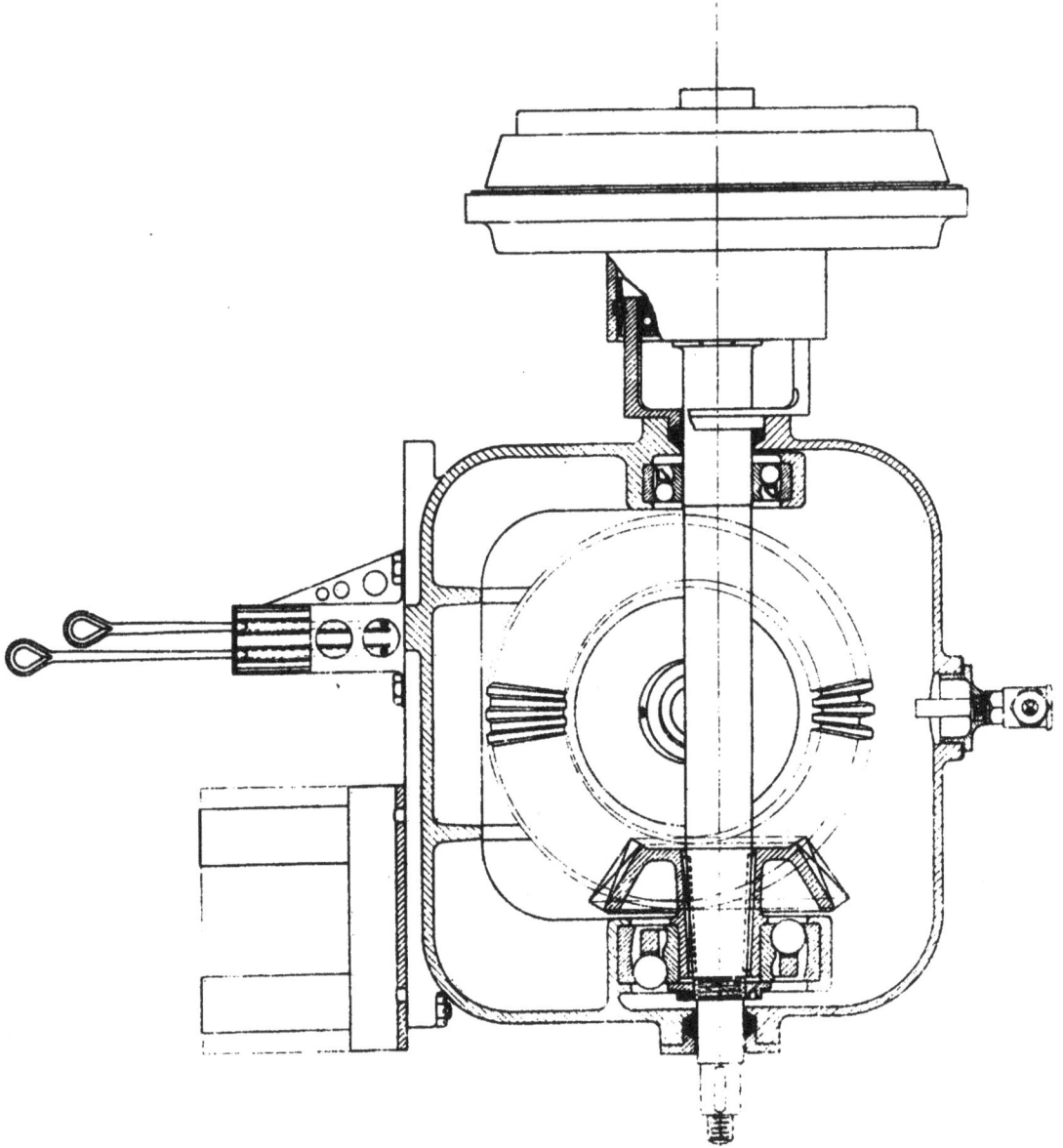

J. III. C & R. L?? W? 7703. 750. 6/19.

FIG. 16

Cross Section through rear driving shaft of Main Gear Box.

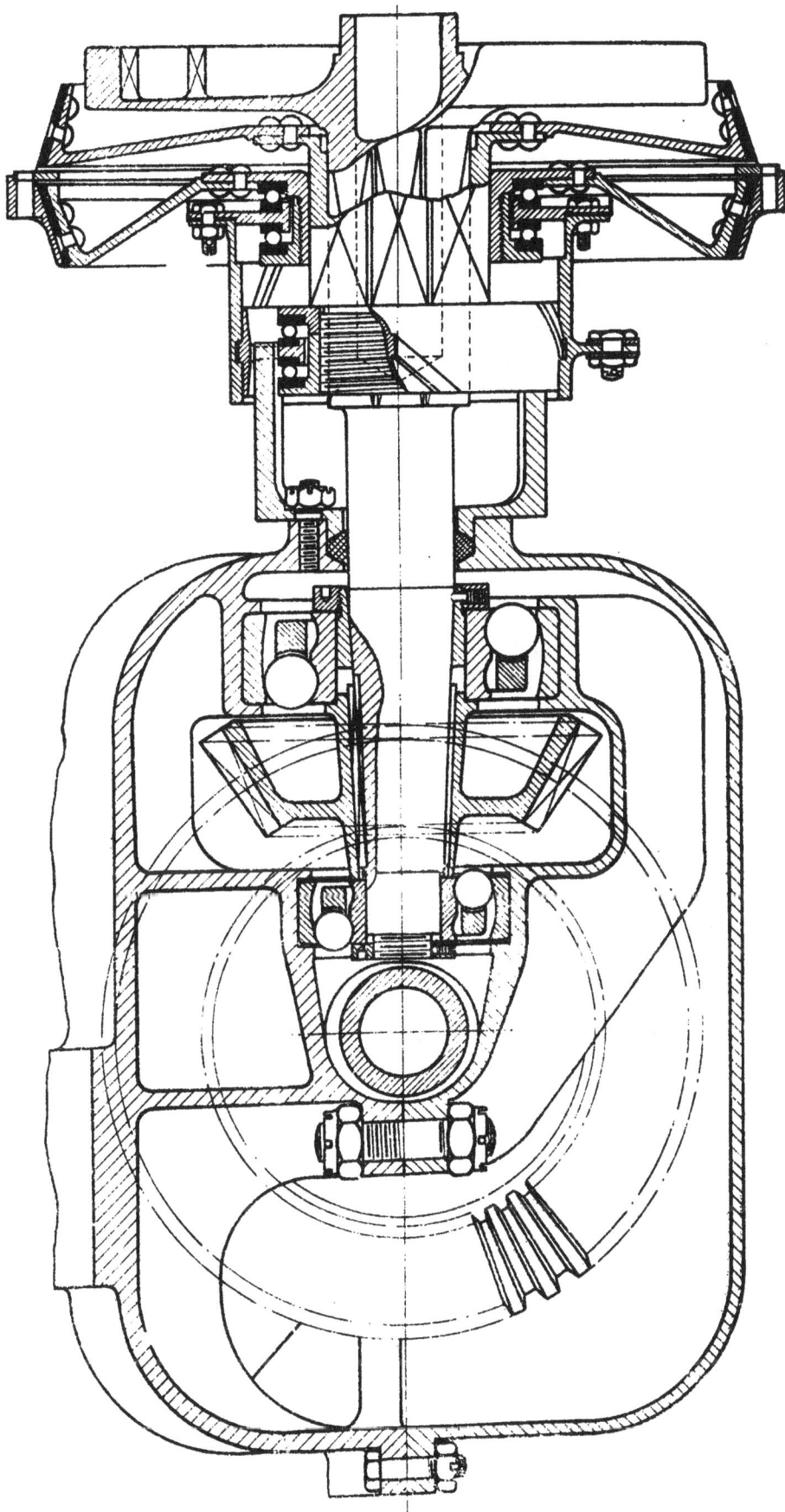

FIG. 17.
Cross Section through forward driving shaft of Main Gear Box.

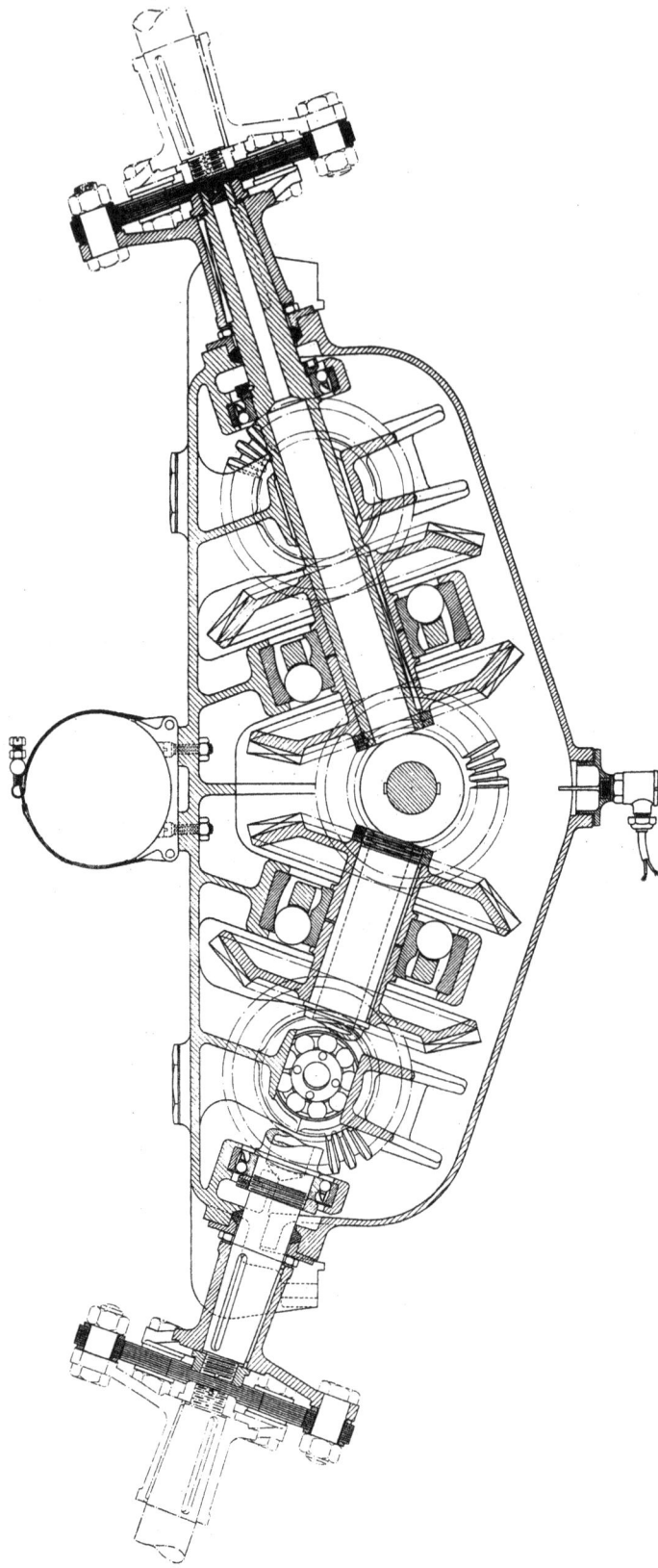

23.

FIG. 18

Cross Section through driven shafts of Main Gear Box.

J. III. C&R L° N° 7703 750. 6/19

www.ingramcontent.com/pod-product-compliance
Lightning Source LLC
Chambersburg PA
CBHW081543090426
42741CB00014BA/3253